S0-EFN-337

Olson, Nathan.
Australia in colors /

c2009.
33305220776912
ca   04/09/10

A+ books

WORLD OF COLORS

Australia in Colors

by Nathan Olson

Consultant: Mark L. Healy, professor
William Rainey Harper College
Palatine, Illinois

Capstone press

Mankato, Minnesota

Yellow road signs warn drivers to watch out for hopping kangaroos in the dry Australian outback. Kangaroos and other wildlife roam free in the outback. Not many people live there.

Koalas live in Australia's eucalyptus trees. They munch on the trees' green leaves. Koalas sleep most of the day. At night, they climb from branch to branch to find more leaves.

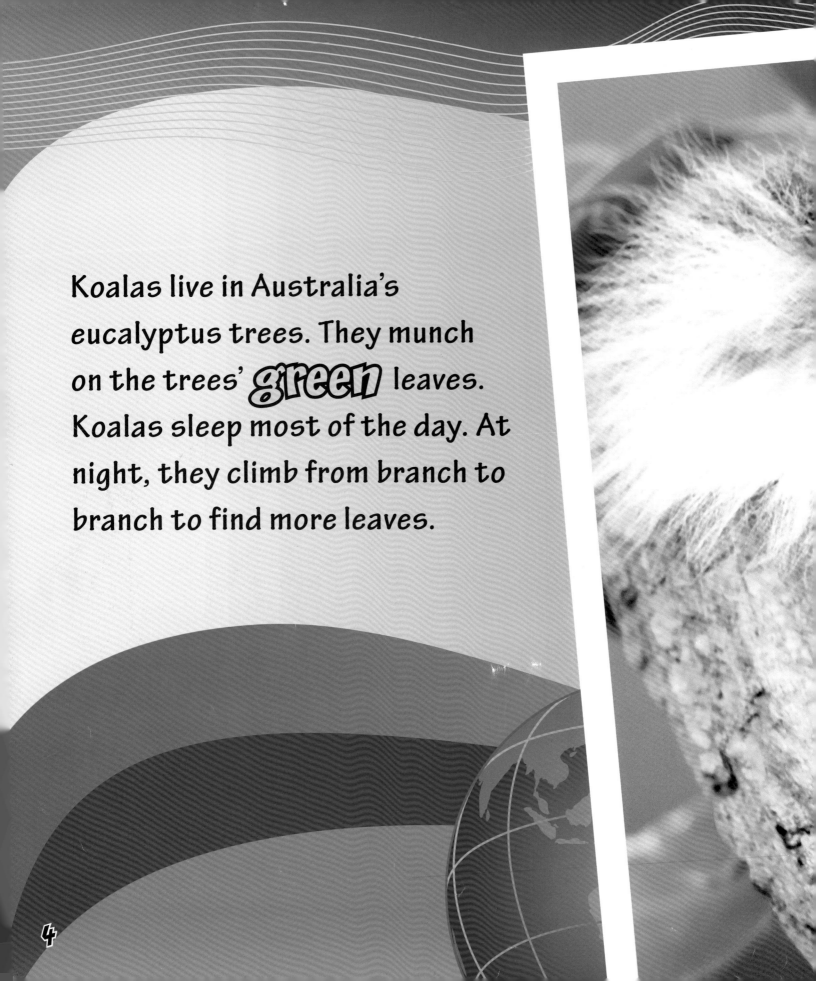

The roof of the Sydney Opera House looks like giant **white** shells. Sydney is the largest city in Australia. About as many people live in Sydney as in the U.S. city of Los Angeles.

Red tiles cover the roofs of many Australian homes. These tiles protect homes from fire. Air blows through spaces between the tiles. Homes stay cool in the hot summer months.

Australia is home to millions of **gray** sheep. In fact, Australia has more sheep than people! Australia produces more wool than any other country in the world.

Australia is bursting with **purple** grapes. They grow in all parts of the country. Grapes are used to make raisins and wine.

The **blue** and **brown** Great Barrier Reef is the largest coral reef on earth. It stretches for more than 1,200 miles (1,931 kilometers) off Australia's northeastern coast. Corals, sea anemones, sea stars, sharks, fish, and giant clams live in the reef.

Orange sandstone on Ayers Rock shines as the sun sets in central Australia. Ayers Rock is also called Uluru. It seems to change color depending on the weather or time of day. It can look purple, orange, or fiery red.

Black, **red**, and **yellow** are the colors of Australia's Aboriginal flag. The black stands for the Aborigine people. They have lived on the continent for more than 40,000 years. The red stands for the earth. The yellow stands for the sun.

Blue uniforms are the dress of the day for these Australian schoolchildren. Students in Australia enjoy their summer vacations in December and January. Seasons in Australia are opposite of those in the northern hemisphere.

Australians celebrate ANZAC Day with memorial wreaths made of **red** poppies. They use poppies to remember fallen soldiers. ANZAC stands for Australian and New Zealand Army Corps. ANZAC Day is Australia's most important national holiday.

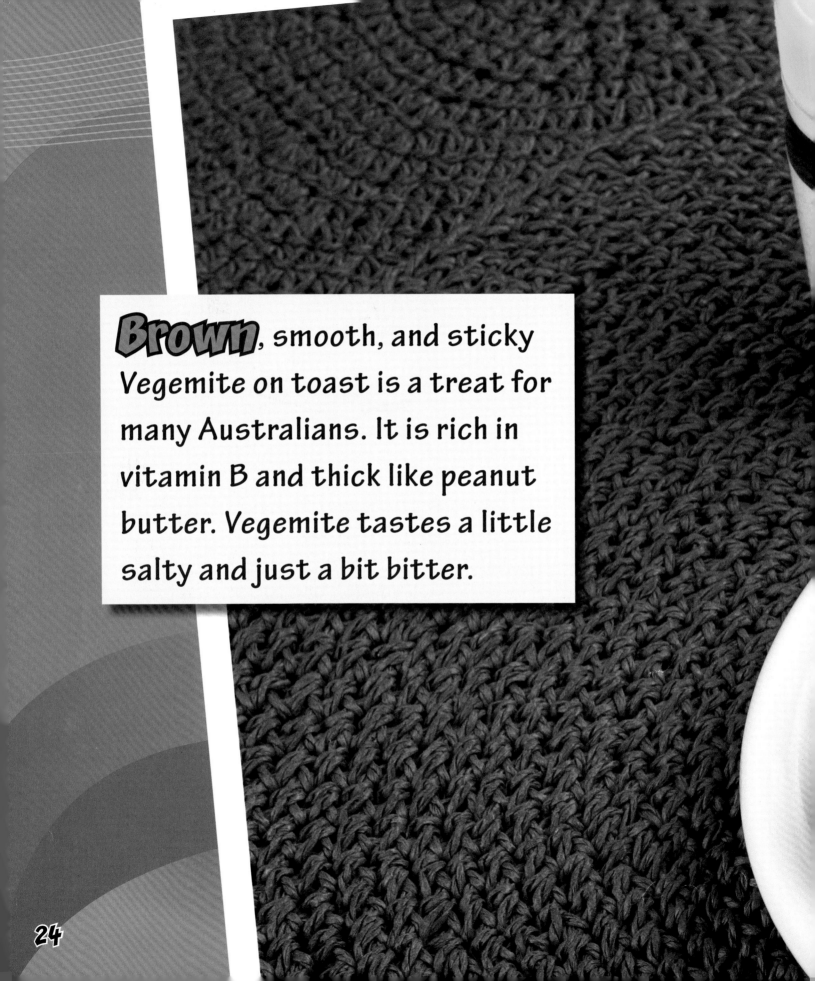

Brown, smooth, and sticky Vegemite on toast is a treat for many Australians. It is rich in vitamin B and thick like peanut butter. Vegemite tastes a little salty and just a bit bitter.

Green and **yellow** cricket uniforms are a common sight in Australia. Cricket is an outdoor bat-and-ball game similar to baseball. Teams take turns at bat and try to score runs.

FACTS about Australia

Capital City: Canberra

Population: 20,600,856

Official Language: English

G'Day, Mate!

Australians speak English, but some of their words are unfamiliar to visitors. A "barbie" isn't a doll — it's an outdoor barbecue. An "eskie" is a cooler that holds ice or soft drinks. A "lollie" is candy. Can you guess what a "prezzie" is? That's right — a present!

Map

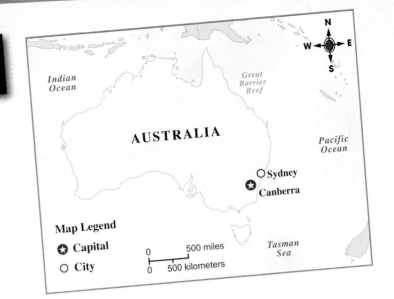

Flag

Money

Australian money is called the Australian dollar. One dollar equals 100 cents.

Glossary

Aborigine (ab-uh-RIJ-uh-nee) — one of the native peoples of Australia who has lived there since before Europeans arrived

continent (KAHN-tuh-nuhnt) — one of the seven large land areas of earth; Australia is the smallest continent.

coral reef (KOR-uhl REEF) — a type of land made up of the hardened bodies of corals; corals are small, colorful sea creatures.

cricket (KRI-kuht) — an outdoor bat-and-ball game that is similar to baseball

eucalyptus (yoo-kuh-LIP-tuhs) — a tree that grows in dry climates; koalas eat eucalyptus leaves.

hemisphere (HEM-uhss-fihr) — one half of the earth; Australia is in the earth's southern hemisphere.

outback (OUT-bak) — the flat desert areas of Australia; not many people live in the outback.

poppy (POP-ee) — a garden plant with large red flowers

sandstone (SAND-stohn) — a kind of rock made of sandlike grains of quartz

Vegemite (VEJ-ih-mite) — a brown, creamy spread made from yeast

Read More

McCollum, Sean. *Australia.* Country Explorers. Minneapolis: Lerner, 2008.

Richardson, Adele. *Australia.* My First Look at Countries. Mankato, Minn.: Creative Education, 2007.

Internet Sites

FactHound offers a safe, fun way to find Internet sites related to this book. All of the sites on FactHound have been researched by our staff.

Here's how:

1. Visit *www.facthound.com*

2. Choose your grade level.

3. Type in this book ID **1429616970** for age-appropriate sites. You may also browse subjects by clicking on letters, or by clicking on pictures and words.

4. Click on the **Fetch It** button.

FactHound will fetch the best sites for you!

Index

32

A+ Books are published by Capstone Press,
151 Good Counsel Drive, P.O. Box 669, Mankato, Minnesota 56002.
www.capstonepress.com

Copyright © 2009 by Capstone Press, a Capstone Publishers company. All rights reserved.
No part of this publication may be reproduced in whole or in part, or stored in a retrieval system,
or transmitted in any form or by any means, electronic, mechanical, photocopying, recording, or
otherwise, without written permission of the publisher. For information regarding permission, write
to Capstone Press, 151 Good Counsel Drive, P.O. Box 669, Dept. R, Mankato, Minnesota 56002.
Printed in the United States of America

1 2 3 4 5 6 13 12 11 10 09 08

Library of Congress Cataloging-in-Publication Data
Olson, Nathan.
   Australia in colors / by Nathan Olson.
     p. cm. — (A+ books. World of colors)
   Summary: "Simple text and striking photographs present Australia, its culture,
and its geography" — Provided by publisher.
   Includes bibliographical references and index.
   ISBN-13: 978-1-4296-1697-3 (hardcover)
   ISBN-10: 1-4296-1697-0 (hardcover)
     1. Australia — Juvenile literature. 2. Australia — Pictorial works — Juvenile literature.
I. Title. II. Series.
DU96.O475 2009
994 — dc22   2008005268

Credits
Megan Peterson, editor; Veronica Bianchini, designer; Wanda Winch, photo researcher

Photo Credits
Art Life Images/age fotostock/Andoni Canela, 2–3; Capstone Press/Karon Dubke,
12–13, 24–25; Getty Images Inc./The Image Bank/Pete Turner, 8–9; Getty Images
Inc./Lonely Planet Images/Michael Coyne, 10–11; Getty Images Inc./Matt King,
26–27; Getty Images Inc./National Geographic/Annie Griffiths Belt, 20–21; Getty
Images Inc./Scott Barbour, 23; iStockphoto/Amanda Rohde, 18–19; iStockphoto/
KJA Photo, 14–15; Photodisc, cover; Shutterstock/Ilya Genkin, 6–7; Shutterstock/
Max Blain, 29 (banknotes); Shutterstock/pxlar8, 4–5; Shutterstock/Robyn Mackenzie,
29 (coins); Shutterstock/Ronald Sumners, 16–17; Shutterstock/WizData, Inc., 1;
StockHaus Ltd., 29 (flag)

Note to Parents, Teachers, and Librarians
This World of Colors book uses full-color photographs and a nonfiction format
to introduce children to basic topics in the study of countries. *Australia in Colors*
is designed to be read aloud to a pre-reader or to be read independently by an
early reader. Photographs help listeners and early readers understand the text
and concepts discussed. The book encourages further learning by including the
following sections: Facts about Australia, Glossary, Read More, Internet Sites,
and Index. Early readers may need assistance using these features.